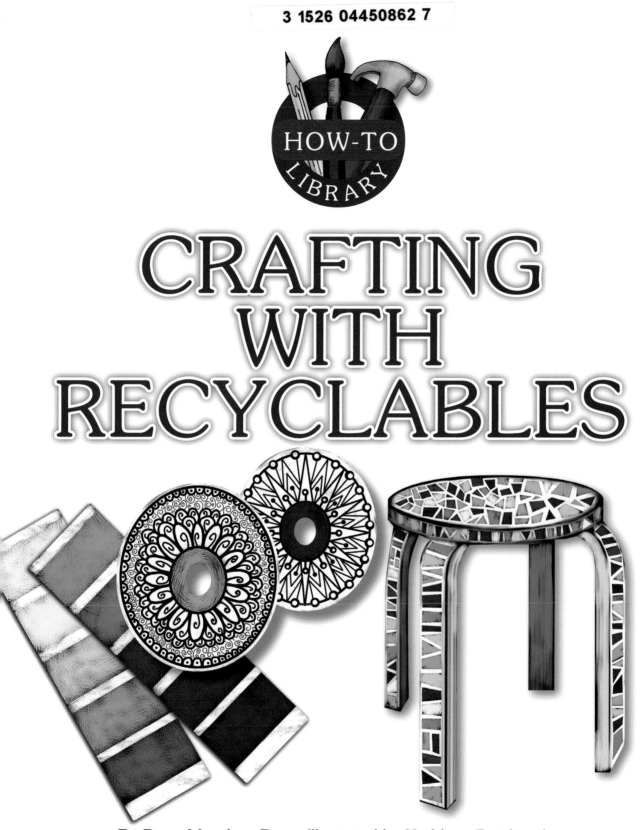

HOW-TO LIBRARY

CRAFTING WITH RECYCLABLES

By Dana Meachen Rau • Illustrated by Kathleen Petelinsek

CHERRY LAKE PUBLISHING • ANN ARBOR, MICHIGAN

CHERRY LAKE
Publishing

A NOTE TO ADULTS:
Please review the instructions for these craft projects before your children make them. Be sure to help them with any steps you do not think they can safely do on their own.

A NOTE TO KIDS:
Be sure to ask an adult for help with these craft activities when you need it. Always put your safety first!

Published in the United States of America by Cherry Lake Publishing
Ann Arbor, Michigan
www.cherrylakepublishing.com

Content Adviser: Dr. Julia Hovanec, Department of Arts Education and Crafts, Kutztown University of Pennsylvania, Kutztown, Pennsylvania

Photo Credits: Page 4, ©Sonya Etchison/Dreamstime.com; page 5, ©Raluca Tudor/Dreamstime.com; page 6, ©Huguette Roe/Shutterstock, Inc.; page 7, ©Morgan Lane Photography/Shutterstock, Inc.; page 8, ©ampyang/Shutterstock, Inc.; page 9, ©Paul McKinnon/Shutterstock.com; pages 24 and 26, ©Dana Meachen Rau; page 29, ©Diego Cervo/Shutterstock, Inc.

Library of Congress Cataloging-in-Publication Data
Rau, Dana Meachen, 1971–
   Crafting with recyclables / by Dana Meachen Rau.
       pages cm. — (How-to library) (Crafts)
   Audience: Grade 4 to 6.
   Includes bibliographical references and index.
   ISBN 978-1-62431-146-8 (library binding) — ISBN 978-1-62431-278-6 (paperback) — ISBN 978-1-62431-212-0 (e-book) 1. Handicraft—Juvenile literature. 2. Recycling (Waste, etc.)—Juvenile literature. I. Title.

TT171.R38 2013
745.5—dc23   2013009785

Cherry Lake Publishing would like to acknowledge the work of The Partnership for 21st Century Skills. Please visit www.p21.org for more information.

Printed in the United States of America
Corporate Graphics Inc.
July 2013
CLFA13

TABLE OF CONTENTS

One of a Kind

Life would be boring if everyone were the same. How do you stand out from the crowd? Think of the hobbies and sports you enjoy that make you unique. Think about your interests, sense of humor, or beliefs. The combination of all these things makes you one of a kind!

You can make one-of-a-kind crafts that reflect your unique personality. One good way to do this is with recycled materials.

Everyone has different interests and ideas, which make them unique.

Many of the things people throw away can be used for interesting craft projects.

Look around your home, school, and community at the items people normally throw in the trash. Some things you find in the trash, such as banana peels, are definitely garbage. But is the lid of a jar garbage? Or the ribbons from your birthday presents? What could you do with the pictures on an outdated calendar? All of these things can be transformed into something new. The creation you make from them will be different from items you buy in a store. It will be a unique creation of your own!

Too Much Trash

People in the United States throw away about 250 million tons (227 million metric tons) of trash every year.

What happens to the trash you put out on the curb, toss in a dumpster, or bring to the dump? It goes to a landfill. A landfill is a place where trash is buried and layered with soil so that it will **decompose**. But some items can be recycled.

Recycling means reusing an item again. Paper, glass, metal, and plastic can all be recycled. Some towns and cities have centers where these materials are collected. The recycling center prepares them to be sent to places where they can be remade into new products. Paper can be shredded, mixed with water, and made into new types of paper. Metal, glass, and plastic can be melted and remolded into new forms.

You can play a part in recycling, too. If you use recyclables as craft supplies, you are reusing them in a unique way. Sometimes artists call this "upcycling."

Recycling helps reduce the amount of trash that goes into landfills.

THE RECYCLING SYMBOL
Recycling bins are often marked with a picture of three arrows in a triangle shape. This is the universal symbol of recycling. This symbol can also be found on packages, jars, containers, and other items that can be recycled or that are made out of recycled materials.

Endless Supplies

Where can you find items to recycle into craft projects? Here are some ideas:

Around the House

Check in the kitchen, where you might find plastic lids, bottle caps, cardboard boxes, mesh onion bags, and more. Look in the closet for clothing that is worn-out or too small. Neckties, T-shirts, buttons, sweaters, or socks with holes can all be used to create new projects. Magazines, newspapers, wrapping paper, nubs of crayons, or scraps of string can be reused, too. Even lint from the clothes dryer makes good stuffing! Be creative and go on a recycling scavenger hunt.

Search your closet for old clothes you don't wear anymore.

You can find all sorts of inexpensive supplies at tag sales.

Tag Sales

People in your neighborhood might hold tag sales in their front yard or driveway. These sales allow families to sell things they don't need or want anymore. Tag sales are great places to get furniture, old board games, books, or other household items at low prices.

Friends and Family

Ask your friends or family members if they have any items to share. Encourage them to not only help clean up the world by recycling but also clean up their homes. Perhaps you can offer to help them clean out a closet, basement, or attic in exchange for any treasures you might find that you can use for a craft project.

Basic Tools

Projects need different supplies and materials. Here is a list of some of the basic items you will need for the projects in this book.

Cutting Tools

Paper scissors work best for most projects. Fabric scissors are a little sharper. They will help you cut through fabric and ribbon. A box cutter can cut deep into thicker materials. Never use a box cutter without the help of an adult. It is very sharp. Even if you are being careful, it can hurt you.

Tape and Glue

Tape and glue are **adhesives**. There are many different kinds. For the gift card chandelier (*see page 24*), you will use electrical tape. This is a **flexible** vinyl tape that is safe for electronic projects. For the stool decorated with paint samples (*see page 20*) and the secret treasure book box (*see page 26*) you will use varnish. Varnish is a type of glue that hardens to a clear finish after you paint it onto an object.

Sewing Supplies

You will need a needle, thread, and straight pins. Use pins with large colorful heads. They are easier to grip and easier to find on the floor if they fall!

Drawing Supplies

Keep paper and pencils handy for making plans or patterns. You can also jot down or sketch ideas for future projects.

Appliances and Tools

For some of the projects in this book, you will need a blender, electrical drill, hanging light kit, and washing machine. Always ask an adult for permission and help when using these tools and appliances. Never use them alone.

Recyclable Materials

The list of possible materials is endless! You can use paper, metal, glass, and plastic—the items that normally go into a recycling bin. But recycled materials can be anything you reuse. In this book, you will use the following:

- Scraps of ribbon, lace, and construction paper
- Paint samples
- An old piece of furniture
- An old wool sweater and T-shirt
- Old CDs or DVDs
- An old lamp shade
- An old book
- Used plastic gift cards

Painting and Sewing Tips

Painting

You'll be doing two kinds of painting in this book. Acrylic paint is a good way to add pizzazz to recycled materials. Decoupage (pronounced day-koo-PAHZH) is the craft technique of gluing paper to another surface, such as glass or wood, with varnish. Here are some tips for painting and decoupage:

- Keep things neat. Spread newspapers over your work surface to catch any drips. Wear an apron or smock to protect your clothes.
- Use a paper plate as a **palette** to hold your paint or varnish. When you are done, you can just throw it away or recycle it into a new craft.
- Clean your brush in warm, soapy water immediately after you are done. Water-based paints and varnishes make cleanup a lot easier.
- Sometimes you might need to use more than one coat of paint or varnish.

Sewing

Sewing is a great way to attach fabric, ribbon, or other soft materials to a craft project.

Threading a needle: Make sure you have good lighting. Hold the needle steady as you poke the thread through the eye of the needle. You may have to try a few times! Pull the thread through until the two ends meet. Then tie them in a knot. Now you won't have to worry about the thread slipping off the needle.

Running stitch: This is a basic in-and-out stitch. Poke the needle down into the fabric and pull it until it stops at the knot. Then poke the needle up through the fabric and pull all the way through. Repeat until you reach the end. Try to keep your stitches straight and even.

Securing the end: When you reach the end of the fabric, poke the needle in and out again very close together, but don't pull it all the way through yet. Instead, poke the needle through the loop made by the thread. Then pull it all the way through. Repeat to make a double knot. Trim off the extra thread with fabric scissors.

Flashy Flower
Sun Catcher

Sun catchers will
brighten every room!

Do you need a way to reuse old CDs or DVDs?
Try hanging them in a window. The sparkly
sides catch the sun and light up in rainbow colors.

Materials
- An old CD or DVD
- Fine-tip and broad-tip permanent black markers
- Acrylic paint in various colors
- Paintbrushes in various sizes
- Paper plate palette
- Invisible thread
- Scissors

ACRYLIC PAINT

Steps

1. Doodle shapes or draw a pattern of repeating shapes and lines all over the shiny surface of the disc with the markers. Be creative! There are no rules for creating your pattern.

2. Flip the disc over, and paint the other side with a bright color of acrylic paint. Let it dry.

3. Cut a long piece of invisible thread. Thread it through the center hole of the disc. Loop it around and tie it at the edge of the disc with a knot. Tie another knot at the end of the thread.

4. Hang your sun catcher in a sunny window to catch some rays!

MAKING A MOBILE

Try combining several sun catchers to make a mobile. Tie the threads of three or more sun catchers side by side on a stick or rod. Then use invisible thread to hang up the rod.

T-Shirt Makeover

Make an old T-shirt into a fun fashion statement. Ask a friend, parent, or other family member who sews if they have any beads or scraps of ribbon or lace that you can use to add some flair to your project.

Materials
- An old T-shirt
- Scraps of ribbon and lace
- Plastic beads
- Fabric scissors
- Pins
- Needle and thread
- Fabric markers (optional)

Steps
1. Lay the T-shirt flat on your work surface. Trim off the **hems** of the sleeves and the shirt bottom. Cut each arm hem into one strip. Cut the bottom hem into two strips.
2. Sew a running stitch along the edge of one of the strips. When you reach the end, pull the thread so that the fabric scrunches up like an accordion. Roll it into a **coil** so that it

looks like a rose. Sew the bottom of the rose closed and secure it with a knot.

3. Repeat this step with the other strips so that you have four roses.

4. Sew a piece of ribbon or lace around the shirt's neckline. Sew the fabric roses along the neckline, too.

5. Pin a wider ribbon or piece of lace on the back of the shirt a few inches below the armholes. Secure it to the shirt with a running stitch on the top and bottom edge. You will tie this ribbon in the front when you wear the shirt.

6. Fold each sleeve in half. Cut small triangle shapes along the folded edge. When you unfold the sleeve, you will have a diamond pattern.

7. Cut evenly spaced strips along the bottom of the shirt to make fringe. Decorate the fringe with beads, and then knot the end of each strip. You can also add designs by drawing on your shirt with fabric markers. The final design is up to you!

front

back

Scrap Paper Bowl

If you are a crafty person, you probably have lots of paper scraps left over from other projects. Instead of throwing them away, transform them into a colorful bowl. Construction paper works well for this project because it breaks down easily. But you can use scraps of newspaper, too.

Materials

- Scraps of construction paper
- Scissors
- Measuring cup
- Blender
- Water
- Spoon
- Strainer
- Paper towels
- A small bowl that fits snugly inside the strainer
- Dry kitchen sponge

Steps

1. Cut the scraps of construction paper into 1-inch (2.5-centimeter) squares. You need about a cup of them. Place them in the blender. Add a cup of water to the blender. Blend the water and paper together until it becomes a mushy **pulp**.

2. Working over the sink, spoon the pulp into the strainer. With the back of a spoon, try to push all the water you can through the strainer into the sink. As you push the water out, spread the pulp around the strainer so that it is an even thickness all around.

3. Place a few layers of paper towel down on the kitchen counter. Place a small bowl upside down on top of them. Wrap the bowl in another piece of paper towel.

4. Flip the strainer upside down onto the bowl. Use a dry sponge to press all over the bottom of the strainer, absorbing as much water as you can.

5. Lift the strainer carefully from the pulp. Let the paper bowl sit for about 24 hours to dry completely.

A UNIQUE LOOK
Try adding glitter, pine needles, or dryer lint when you blend your paper pulp together. This will give your project a unique look.

Paint Sample Stool

You may have an old stool or other piece of furniture around your house that needs a colorful pick-me-up. Cut up old paint samples and decoupage them onto the stool. Soon you'll be sitting pretty!

Materials

- An old stool or other small piece of furniture
- Sandpaper
- Paint and paintbrush (optional)
- Many colorful paint samples
- Scissors
- Sponge brush
- Water-based varnish
- Paper plate palette

Steps

1. Sand the stool with sandpaper to help smooth out **imperfections** and remove old paint or varnish. Be sure to sand in the direction of the wood grain, not against it. If the surface

still has a lot of old paint, you can repaint the stool white or any color you want. Let it dry completely before moving to step 2.

2. Cut the paint samples into small squares or other shapes. Pour some varnish onto your paper plate palette. Use a sponge brush to paint some varnish onto the top of the stool. Place a color square on top. Then paint over the square with varnish.

3. Repeat with more squares all over the top of the stool. You can overlap them if you want. When the surface is covered, paint all over the top of the stool again with a coat of varnish.

4. Repeat steps 2 and 3 on the legs of your stool if you want.

5. Let the stool dry for about 2 hours or until it is dry to the touch. Then add a second coat of varnish all over the top and legs. Let the stool dry for at least 24 hours before you use it.

THICK AND THIN

Paint samples are made on thick paper, so they work best on completely flat surfaces. If your stool or piece of furniture has rounded legs, you may want to use thinner paper, such as recycled office paper, wrapping paper, or tissue paper.

Easy-to-Make Mittens

If you wash a wool sweater in a washing machine, it will shrink. This is not good for your favorite sweater, but it is just what you want to do for this project! Shrink an old sweater into a feltlike material. Then use the new fabric to make mittens.

Materials
- Old wool sweater (must be 100 percent wool, not washable wool)
- Washing machine, laundry soap, and towel
- Pencil, paper, and scissors
- Fabric scissors
- Pins
- Needle and thread

Steps
1. Place the sweater in a washing machine. Wash it at the hottest setting with a little bit of laundry soap. It will shrink into a tight fabric. If you can still see individual knitted stitches on the sweater, wash it again. Lay it out on a towel to dry completely.

2. Trace a mitten shape around your hand on a piece of paper. Draw the line about ½ inch (1.3 cm) larger than your hand. Cut out the shape with scissors. This is your pattern.

3. Pin your pattern onto the sweater fabric. Use fabric scissors to cut out the fabric. Repeat three more times so that you have four mitten shapes in all.

4. Match up two of the shapes right sides together. Use a needle and thread to sew from the wrist, around the thumbhole, around the top, and back to the other wrist end. Secure the thread with a knot. Leave the bottom of the mitten open.

5. Turn the mitten right side out.

6. Repeat steps 4 and 5 with the other two mitten shapes.

Gift Card Chandelier

Gift cards are popular presents for birthdays and holidays. But they get thrown away after all the money on them is used up. Collect your old cards, and ask friends and family to do the same. Visit tag sales to find an old lamp shade. You can find a hanging light kit at most hardware stores. It consists of a socket on the end of an electrical cord.

Materials
- Old lamp shade with **diameter** of 10 to 12 inches (25 to 30 cm)
- Hanging light kit (use a bulb marked "CFL" or "LED")
- Black electrical tape
- About 45 gift cards
- Electric hand drill with ⅛-inch (3 millimeter) bit
- Thin black ribbon
- Scissors

Steps
1. Remove all of the fabric or other material from the lamp shade until you are left with just the top metal frame. Ask an adult to help you attach your hanging light kit to the lamp shade frame.

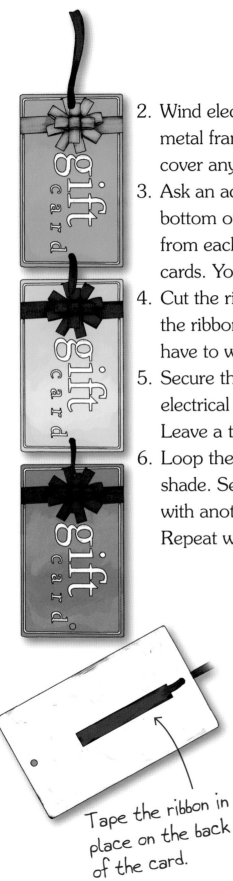

2. Wind electrical tape around the metal frame of the lamp shade to cover any imperfections.

3. Ask an adult to drill holes in the top and bottom of each gift card, about ¼ inch (6 mm) from each edge. Plan how you will arrange your cards. You will need three rows of cards.

4. Cut the ribbon into 12-inch (30 cm) lengths. Thread the ribbon in and out through the holes. You don't have to weave out through the last hole.

5. Secure the ribbon to the back of each card with electrical tape. Trim the bottom end of the ribbon. Leave a tail at the top.

6. Loop the top tail of ribbon over the rim of the lamp shade. Secure the ribbon to the back of the top card with another piece of tape. Trim the extra ribbon. Repeat with the rest of the cards and ribbon.

Tape the ribbon in place on the back of the card.

HOW TO HANG YOUR CHANDELIER

To hang your new light from the ceiling, you will need two hooks. Have an adult screw them into the ceiling—one goes above the outlet where you will plug in your lamp. The other one goes over the area you want to light up. Hang your light on these hooks. Secure the cord to the hooks with twist ties if it slips.

Secret Treasure Book Box

Do you need a place to keep something special? Make a box out of an old book. Place it on your shelf with a bunch of other books. No one will know where you've hidden your secret treasures! Since you will be using a box cutter, ask an adult to help with this project.

Materials

- A thick book with a hard cover (make sure it is an old book that no one wants to read anymore!)
- Ruler
- Pencil
- Box cutter
- Large binder clip
- Water-based varnish
- Sponge brush
- Paper plate palette

Steps

1. Open your book and measure a frame with at least a 1-inch (2.5 cm) border on the first page.

2. Hold the ruler along the lines of the frame. Use the box cutter to cut around the frame as deep as you can through the pages. Remove the paper from inside the frame.

3. Clip the cut pages to the book's front cover to keep them out of the way. Use one of the cut pages as a guide to cut through the next bunch of pages, again using a ruler to keep the lines straight. Try to keep all of the pages lined up together as a block.

4. Repeat step 3 until you have cut through most of the pages, leaving about ½ inch (1.3 cm) of pages at the end of the book.

5. Next you will glue down all the pages, starting from the back of the book. Using a paper plate as a palette to hold the varnish, dip your sponge brush in the varnish. Spread it on the inside of the back cover. Press down the last page onto the back cover.

6. For every ¼ inch (6 mm) of pages, paint a page with varnish. Cover the entire surface. Press down the pages after it. Continue until you reach the framed pages.

7. Spread varnish all around the frame, and press down the pages in sections, as in step 6. Do not spread varnish on the first page. (You don't want it to stick to the front cover—the front cover needs to be able to open like a lid.)

8. Close the book and make sure all of the pages are lined up in a block. Paint around the three sides of the block of pages generously with varnish. Make sure the top cover can still open, wiping off any varnish that may make it stick. Then close the book tightly and seal it with rubber bands. Let it sit for about an hour as the varnish dries and hardens.

9. Open the book's cover. Spread varnish all around the frame of the first page and the sides and bottom of the hole. Spread a second coat of varnish around the sides of the book block. Let the varnish dry completely with the front cover open.

Do Your Part— Together!

Host a recycling party! Make invitations with scraps of paper from magazines, wrapping paper, or old gift cards. Invite your friends to your home to make crafts. Ask them to bring recyclable materials. Share ideas and supplies. Let your imaginations fly!

You are helping the earth when you recycle. You are reducing the amount of trash in landfills. When you turn those recyclable materials into crafts, you are doing something else important for the earth, too. You are making it a little more beautiful with a unique contribution to the world!

Recycling is a great way to help keep the planet healthy.

Glossary

adhesives (ad-HEE-sivz) substances, such as glue, that make things stick together

coil (KOIL) a loop or series of loops

decompose (dee-kuhm-POZE) to break down into soil

diameter (dye-AM-uh-tur) a straight line through the center of a circle, connecting opposite sides

flexible (FLEK-suh-buhl) able to bend

hems (HEMZ) edges of material that have been folded over and sewn down

imperfections (im-pur-FEK-shuhnz) faults or mistakes

palette (PAL-uht) a flat board that is used for mixing paints

pulp (PUHLP) any soft, wet mixture

recycling (ree-SYE-kling) preparing old items, such as glass, plastic, newspapers, and aluminum cans, to be made into new products

For More Information

Books

Enz, Tammy. *Repurpose It: Invent New Uses for Old Stuff*. Mankato, MN: Capstone Press, 2012.

Friday, Megan. *Green Crafts: Become an Earth-Friendly Craft Star, Step by Easy Step!* Irvine, California: Walter Foster Pub., 2011.

Gardner, Robert. *Recycle: Green Science Projects for a Sustainable Planet*. Berkeley Heights, NJ: Enslow Publishers, 2011.

Rau, Dana Meachen. *Plastic*. New York: Marshall Cavendish Benchmark, 2012.

Scheunemann, Pam. *Cool Odds and Ends Projects: Creative Ways to Upcycle Your Trash into Treasure*. Minneapolis: ABDO Publishing Company, 2013.

Web Sites

Environmental Protection Agency: Recycle City

www.epa.gov/recyclecity

Learn about the many ways a community can cut down on landfill waste.

Spoonful— Recycled Crafts Projects for Kids Gallery

http://spoonful.com/create/recyclable-crafts-gallery

Browse this collection of fun ideas for recyclable crafts.

Index

About the Author

Dana Meachen Rau is the author of more than 300 books for children on many topics, including science, history, cooking, and crafts. She creates, experiments, researches, and writes from her home office in Burlington, Connecticut.